Oneness
The Pearls

A Treasury of Divine Wisdom

Also by Rasha

Books:
Oneness

A Journey to Oneness

The Calling

Audio:
Oneness

*The Meditations of Oneness:
A Journey to the Heart of the Divine Lover*

All of the above may be ordered by visiting:
www.onenesswebsite.com

Oneness
The Pearls
A Treasury of Divine Wisdom

Rasha

Earthstar Press
369 Montezuma Ave. #321
Santa Fe, New Mexico 87501
USA

www.onenesswebsite.com

Contact: onenessmailbox@gmail.com

© 2015 Rasha

All rights reserved. No part of this book may be reproduced, stored, transmitted or otherwise copied – other than as brief quotations embodied in articles and reviews – without prior written permission of the publisher.

This book offers information of a general nature to support your quest for emotional and spiritual well-being. Should you choose to use any of the information in this book, the author and the publisher assume no responsibility for your actions.

ISBN-13: 978-0-9659003-6-2

Cover image: "Pearl" by Vladimir Kush
www.vladimirkush.com

Book & cover design by S. Janarthanan

First edition: 2015

Printed in India

Contents

Introduction *8*

1. *The Journey Begins* *11*
2. *Shifting Old Patterns* *23*
3. *Transformation* *37*
4. *Harmony & Relationship* *47*
5. *Experiencing your Emotions* *61*
6. *Trust & Surrender* *71*
7. *Embracing Change* *81*
8. *Ascension* *89*
9. *Who Am I?* *101*

Contents

10. Leaving the Past Behind 109

11. The Call of Divine Intent 117

12. Creating your Reality 125

13. Honoring your Inner Truth 135

14. Your Spiritual Path 147

15. Unity with Diversity 159

16. The Artist & The Dreamer 169

17. The Journey Home. 177

18. Compassion. 191

19. You are Oneness 199

20. Enlightenment. 211

Introduction

The volume you hold in your hands is a virtual passport for a most extraordinary journey. Here, in these pages, you'll find a treasure trove of Divine wisdom, the core concepts culled from the life-changing spiritual classic I was privileged to receive and transcribe, entitled *Oneness*. This book is your personal invitation to actually embark on the journey of a lifetime you've always told yourself you'd make, someday. Someday has arrived.

In February 1998, I began a profound dialogue with the universal Presence I came to know as "Oneness" – the Divinity we all share and many people refer to as "God." Word for word, over the course of years, I documented the principles for another level of understanding of the mystery we think of as "life." These teachings empower us to take a quantum leap into our own inner depths and totally transform our lives – and our world.

Here, in these words of wisdom, we discover clues that inspire us to create the kinds of lives we long for, and help us release the energies that prevent us from realizing our dreams. We learn to recognize the emotional patterns that undermine our best intentions. And we start to harmonize with the powerful energies building all around us – and with the power of Creation that's driving it.

My own inner journey with the Oneness material opened doors within me I never dreamed existed. It was as though the Messages tucked in those pages had a destiny all their own. I was astonished to discover that, ready or not, I'd embarked on the proverbial journey of a lifetime, and began to recognize my own life experiences as living illustrations of the life-changing concepts I'd documented. I realized that I hadn't just received and transcribed the book, *Oneness* – I was literally living it!

I soon discovered that I was in very good company. The phenomenon of watching the concepts in the book, *Oneness*, coming to life before my very eyes, is one that's been described again and again in letters from readers from all over the world. I came to understand that there are encodements, seeded within the Oneness material, which can serve to bring the teachings to life for each reader. In this way, these powerful concepts are instilled within us as "knowingness," drawn from our own personal experience of them, rather than just philosophical ideas to grasp with our minds.

Over the years, I discovered hundreds of timeless aphorisms within those pages – powerful, self-contained nuggets of wisdom, often referred to as "sutras" amongst certain spiritual traditions of the East. Over time, I began sharing these aphorisms with the world, via the internet. Several beautiful e-mail series were created, which added vivid photographic illustrations to the Messages, and brought the wisdom of Oneness to life. Later, posting these modern-day sutras on our two Oneness Facebook pages helped people share concepts they found particularly meaningful with the family and friends they knew needed them the most.

Through it all, the dream of creating a beautifully illustrated volume that captured the very essence of the teachings of Oneness, continued to simmer within me. From the very beginning, I'd created a computer folder where I stashed each aphorism, as I compiled the collection, and had labelled the file, appropriately, "The Pearls." Year by year, the folder continued to grow until it emerged as a virtual treasury of Divine wisdom – a tool for spiritual growth that had essentially created itself – as it awaited its appointed moment in time.

This volume is organized into twenty sections, each focused on a cornerstone of the teachings of Oneness. Each of the timeless sutras you'll find there is a self-contained Message – a powerful reminder, created by the Divine Presence that waits within you, of what you already know, deep inside. These precious words serve as pointers that invite you to stop and consider them. Ponder them. Note the inner direction that begins to beckon to you. And feel the subtle momentum that carries you there.

Take the time to savor these words. Imbibe the message in each of the images. And be prepared to simply let go, and surrender to the impetus from within that comes to take you by the hand to another octave of your own Beingness. That is the gift that awaits you – tucked inside these pearls of wisdom. This book is your invitation to embark on that very special journey of Self-discovery – and ultimately, to embrace who you really Are.

Rasha,
August, 2015

The Journey Begins

*This is the lifetime
that will catapult you beyond all you know
to a depth of awareness and understanding
you are as yet unable to fathom.
Trust that this process is unfolding
as it is meant to.
And that everything is, indeed,
in Divine order.*

*This is the journey
that will carry you the full distance –
beyond the parameters of the entire concept of a lifetime –
to a state of being that is the embodiment of timelessness.
A state of being known as Oneness.*

*You stand at the threshold
of a grand adventure.*

*The extent to which you are able to experience
the fullness of that journey
is determined by the extent to which you are able to let go
of the scenarios that no longer serve you.*

There comes a total shift in focus to heart-centeredness. Your perception of self and that of the world around you become intertwined.

You begin to dance with the energies of life, allowing the ebb and flow to determine the direction.

*As you release
the constraints that
bind you
to circumstances you
have outgrown,
you discover
that the direction
of choice
is found on a road
you must travel
alone.*

*One becomes as a leaf on the wind,
willing to be carried with the momentum of the process,
knowing that one's best interests and well-being
are being seen to in every possible way.*

*There are any number of avenues
to the crossroads
toward which you may be headed
at any given moment.*

*Forgive yourself the misdirected notion
that you have strayed off-track
by letting certain opportunities pass you by.
You will get to where you are going
by any number of alternative means.
It cannot be otherwise.*

You are a multidimensional being.
You are not limited to the particular identity
that you have come to regard as you.
There are viable aspects of self that live, unbeknownst to you,
in parallel realities, who reach out for the lost aspect of self
that you would consider to be you.
To these beings, you are a missing note
in a chord that defines
their very existence.

The common ground and the paths
upon which you will merge, energetically,
with all aspects of self are the emotions you share
at the deepest level.

*This opportunity for reflection
is likely to initiate
a monumental shift within you
that will help you to halt
your conditioned patterns of response –
and be Still.*

Shifting Old Patterns

*The key
to all you would accomplish in this lifetime
hinges upon your willingness to embrace all that you are,
for the chance that you may come to experience – in Oneness –
all that you truly Are.*

*It is not necessary to experience
repeat performances of painful dramas
simply because you have neglected to release the energy charge
carried by those experiences, and express the emotions
they are calculated to trigger.*

*In shifting the energy
you project onto any moment or situation,
you consciously shift the outcome
to one that will give you a more advantageous result.*

*Know that you are
in command of your situation at all times.
You are able to choose to step back, at will,
from the heat of the moment,
and make the conscious choice to shift the energy
to one emanating from the place
of heart-centeredness.*

*When circumstances
deliver you to a state of being
that you recognize to be unbalanced,
take the opportunity to step back for a moment.
Withdraw your energies and cease conscious interaction
with all that surrounds you – all that is external
to the Source of your own being.
And allow your awareness to guide you
to a place of Stillness deep within.*

*A seemingly negative situation may well be the gateway
to the precise shift in focus that will deliver you into the arena
where you can do your life's work.*

*The vibration of every thought pattern
that passes through your consciousness carries an energy charge;
particularly the thought patterns that are materialized
in the form of verbal communication.*

*By releasing an energy charge in the form of speech,
you set into motion an imprint that magnetizes to it
circumstances of a corresponding vibration.
That is what is meant by the expression:
"your thoughts create your reality."*

*Your thought patterns,
even when not expressed verbally,
carry an energy charge that sets in motion
circumstances of a corresponding vibration.*

*Become aware of the time lag
between an emotionally charged response
and the next negatively charged occurrence.
It will become painfully obvious
that there is an indisputable connection
between cause and effect.*

*By being fully conscious of what you are doing
in those moments when you feel those old familiar buttons being pushed,
you can begin to dissipate the vibrational charge that is drawing
those kinds of circumstances to you.*

Spontaneous recall of related incidents in one's life history occurs for everyone, and leads to the identification of a common thread that ties the collection of entwined experiences into a cohesive unit.

You will continue to manifest life circumstances that will put your understandings to the test, long after you have mastered them in theory.

Until issues are ingrained as knowingness to the extent that they become your reflex responses, you will continue to manifest opportunities to strengthen those new patterns of reaction

Maintain a state of balance and heart-centeredness.

Here, in the heart-centered core of your being, the timeless connections with the multidimensional aspects of self will be made manifest. It is here that you will encounter the gateway to reunification with the Oneness that you Are.

*By embodying this training,
your life becomes one directed by intention
rather than the unconscious reflection of happenstance.*

*You do create all of it.
Know that.*

Transformation

*The opportunity for you now
is to breathe new life into the blessed creation of self,
through heart centered focus.
Then, to stand back
and allow that identity the scope of full expression,
without the influence of past beliefs,
feelings of limitation, or any of the dogmas
you have accumulated
in your travels.*

*You have come to this moment in time,
having surmounted so many of the hurdles that were thrown in your path.
Now what remains to be cleared are remnants of learned responses,
which would have you stumble, out of habit,
over brambles that are clearly in view.*

*There is
no place in the
transcendent consciousness
for any of the baggage
you may still be carrying.
All the shoulds and shouldn'ts
that may have dominated
your consciousness,
are to be released
and left at this
crossroads.*

*Your objective now is moving forward.
Anything that does not support that momentum
is a situation you have the opportunity to transcend
by exercising the power of choice.*

*The path before you now
requires a lightness of spirit
that allows for ample freedom of motion.
One must be able to respond to the opportunities presented
without reservation.*

*One needs to be able to move forward,
unbound by considerations that would limit what is possible
in deference to priorities that no longer resonate
with one's highest good.*

*When you are able to recognize
conditioned responses that are rooted in the need
to "win" a given encounter,
you take the first step toward transcending
the sense of separation
with which you have been equipped.*

*So long as you permit the programming of your mind
to dominate every waking breath, and so long as you run your life
as a mindless exercise of reflex responses calculated
to prove that you are "right"
about whatever your issues happen to be,
you will not be capable of experiencing
the exquisite connectedness
that awaits you.*

*Observe that you are now able to just "let it go,"
where once you felt compelled to engage in battle,
and you will begin to see
the process of transcending ego,
in action.*

*Your detachment from the need to be "right"
bears the gift of transcendence.
You will discover within those depths, the Stillness within your own being
that opens the door to your true essence.*

*Until you have nothing left to lose
and nothing left to gain by continuing in your ingrained patterns,
you do not have the catalyst for initiating radical change.*

*So long as you hold your focus in the realm of mundane concerns,
you will be unable to perceive the Divine essence
that calls to you in silence.*

*When you honor your own truth, unconditionally,
it sets the stage for a chain reaction of transformation,
all the way around.*

Harmony & Relationship

*Approach with gentleness and with compassion
the beings with whom you share experience in this time frame.
For, each of you is performing to the very best of his abilities,
playing out roles that have been preordained,
and not without a certain measure of discomfort
all the way around.*

Your objective now is to recognize all encounters as the opportunities for achieving harmony that they truly are.

*In order for harmony truly to be experienced,
there must be the essence of "difference" to comprise it.
There is no harmony in a vacuum.*

*Harmony is dependent upon a recognition of difference
and a willingness to hold one's own truth intact in its presence.*

*When life is working for you,
it cannot be to the detriment of another being.*

*When one ceases to give energy
to the invalidation of the perceptions of another
as a means of reinforcing one's own, one creates the space
for the validity of all variations on a shared vision
and lays the groundwork for the mutual experience of harmony.*

*It is no accident
that some of you are sharing these times with a companion.
You are the ones who have been given the tool of relationship
through which to discover the intimate connection
you share with your own inner being.*

*The recognition of Self in the form of another
is an attestation to the true essence of the very differences
that prove most challenging.
It is evidence of the depth of contrast
without which there can be no harmony.*

*You are here for your journey alone.
And even though you have been provided
the comfort of much camaraderie along the way,
each of you is, in actuality, flying solo
in your "moments of truth."*

*Before real harmony can be experienced
within the context of a relationship,
it is necessary to allow the fullness of the energy
that resonates between you
to be expressed.*

*The key to harmonizing
with the truth of another person's vision
is to hold one's own truth
as a treasure
to be prized, honored
and protected.*

*When two beings share the sacred journey
at an intimate level,
each has been factored in to the growth objective of the other.*

*While you may travel on a parallel path with another
and have certain experiences in common,
your path remains your own.*

*It is far easier to see the flaws
in the thinking and responses of another being
than to see the same in one's self.*

*By presenting
your own perspective
without attachment to outcome,
you allow for the manifestation
of the optimum outcome for all concerned.*

*By planting the seed of your intent – your will –
by presenting your viewpoint
without the need to force it into fruition,
you best serve your own interests
as well as those of the others with whom you are engaged.*

*When potential conflict is nullified
and the intent of each is the harmonization of will,
rather than the manifestation of one's own will over that of another,
the outcome is consistently one that serves
the highest good of all concerned.*

*When you relinquish the need to mastermind
the labyrinth of your existence, and reach deeper to the level
where you can feel rather than think, and know rather than believe,
you will have arrived at the place where you can create a reality
in which you truly move forward.*

*The ability to trust
in the reality that the energy of your world has indeed shifted,
and that there is a higher perspective to be attained,
heralds the turning point
toward which you strive in these times.*

*Once you have tuned-in to the higher resonance
of the harmonization of your personal will with the Will of Creation,
the walls of separation will have dematerialized
and you will come to experience life
as the expression of Unity
that it truly is.*

Experiencing your Emotions

*Profound levels of pain, grief, hurt, disappointment,
and other reactions to the cataclysmic events in your cellular history
now have the opportunity to be revealed to you
through the vehicle of your emotions.*

*It is in your highest possible interests
that you permit yourself the experience of
your emotional responses.*

*As the energies continue to accelerate,
you can expect to experience profound levels of emotional response,
as each life theme, like a chapter unto itself in an ongoing saga,
is permitted to culminate as vivid awareness.
Simultaneously, one can anticipate feeling uninvested
in the outcome of such dramas.*

*Your most profound emotions are being triggered intentionally –
not for the purpose of reinforcing your proficiency in repressing them,
but with the objective of stimulating a profound reaction.*

Allow the episodes of greatest intensity to play out unimpeded.
For, your judgment of the depth of your feelings
could serve to inhibit the authenticity of your response,
should you permit your mind to get in the way.
The objective here is not restraint,
but rather, release.

Each time you complete a poignant episode
and the emotional release of the underlying energy charge
has been achieved, you will be able to see
that it is yet another example
of an experience that has happened
over and over again.

*Recognition
of the underlying theme being represented
does not eliminate the need
for experiential episodes to continue to manifest.
For, it is in the repeated stimulation of the feeling body
that the vibrational release is achieved.*

*Peeling back the layers of experiential density
reveals levels of intensity that lay dormant, often for lifetimes.
As you begin to piece together your core understandings
of the categories of experience you are resolving,
you will have the sense of the timelessness
of some of these themes.*

*These times are about tuning-in fully
to the vibrational history imprinted within you,
and allowing yourself, and the others in your inner circle,
the grace of expressing fully what is represented there.*

*You can anticipate
being taken to the heights and to the depths of
your feeling body's capacity to attune you to the subtle levels
of perception and response.*

*When you encounter
a depth of emotional intensity
that is disproportionate to the incident at hand,
know that it is entirely possible that you have arrived at the point
where past-life energetic patterning is able
to surface and be released.*

*You are not backsliding
simply because you are rehashing issues
that were presumed to have been resolved.
You are progressing perfectly
when you allow the process to reveal to you the last remnants
of energetic patterning, experienced as emotion,
and you allow yourself to feel fully
the depths of the energetic charge
it has been culled forth
to deliver.*

Trust & Surrender

*Permit yourself the luxury
of savoring this experience of transformation.
It is not one to be rushed.
The end result will manifest in its own time,
in a very natural way,
when you allow the process to direct you
and you cease
trying to direct the process.*

*You will be guided from within,
at levels beyond your conscious awareness,
to navigate the depths of some of the experiential rites of passage.
The keywords here are trust and surrender.*

*Trust that there are levels of consciousness within you
that understand precisely what is happening
and why it is necessary that you be subjected to
this period of upheaval.*

*Resist the inclination to judge your own process
or that of others.*

*Each of you is engaged in
the perfection of his own personal journey to Oneness.
And each is contending with an individualized program of experiences
calculated to bring you into the fullness of your capacity
for the transcendence of this level of reality.*

*Your own inner trust,
demonstrated at the times
when your feelings defy your logical mind,
will help you to complete the experiences with ease
and to accomplish the objective
in drawing them to you.*

*Ultimately,
you will begin to notice
the correlation
between your unbridled intent
and the shift in the circumstances
you are able to draw into your life as experience.*

*There will be no doubt
that you have begun to manifest
a different caliber of experience – one that emanates
from a space of inner trust
and contentment.*

*There can be no doubt
of the power of inner peace, made manifest,
which becomes your experience of physical reality.*

*What can be expected from this point forth,
is the magical fluidity of every moment, and the sense of peace
in knowing that your life will never be the same again.*

Embracing Change

*Know that you are most decidedly on track,
despite the sense that life, as you know it, often seems to be derailed.
For, radical change is the order of the day in these times.
This level of change is experienced by everyone
and everything in your physical world.*

*As long as you cling to
the idea of the way "life is supposed to be,"
your life circumstances will continue to reflect a perspective
that sees itself at the effect of circumstances
beyond your control.*

*Life was never meant to be the straight and narrow road
you were taught to envision.*

*This lifetime was preprogrammed with a rich itinerary
of convoluted detours to the destination toward which you travel.
It is the deviation from what you may have expected
that makes this journey fascinating and rewarding
in the ways that really matter.*

*There is no question
in anyone's mind
that unprecedented change is at hand.
The question in the minds of so many
is why – and toward what end –
this momentum propels you.
It is not necessary to understand the process,
much less the overview on a grander scale,
in order to integrate its effects
on a personal level.*

*There are significant changes taking place
in the cellular structure of every life form on your planet
in the present time period.*

The spirit of adventure
has captured the imaginations of many amongst you
who recognize yourselves to be true pioneers
on the border of uncharted territory.
For you, the need to cling to the familiar has given way
to an indisputable sense of being very much on track,
despite evidence to the contrary.

You will look back
upon this time of intensity and upheaval
with a rarefied perspective that is only possible in retrospect.
By that time, you will be able to integrate new levels of perception
into your understanding of what really happened to you in these times,
and why.

Do not expect your life to "return to normal."
That's not what you had in mind when you embarked on this odyssey.
"Normal" is a concept that has no frame of reference
in the realities for which you are preparing.

Ascension

A vast inter-dimensional conversion in consciousness is presently transpiring throughout Creation.

*You are the embodiment of a momentum
that is surging toward the completion of a timeless process.*

*That process is the reunification of all that you are,
all that you have ever been, and all that you are yet to be,
in a simultaneous expression of Oneness.*

*In the simultaneous momentum that drives all aspects of self,
all are able to embody the expanded perspective of higher consciousness.
And all, in unison, become part of the momentum
that is known as "ascension."*

*Ascension is not an "event" but rather, a momentum.
It is a shift in awareness, a shift in perspective, a shift in vibration,
a shift in attunement, and a shift in conscious alignment
with who one truly is.*

*Ascension is a universal motion, a yearning, a striving,
a releasing, a surrendering – a joyous culmination
of your journey here in physical form.*

The motion of ascension is perpetual motion.
And the process has been ongoing since the beginning of Creation.
In these times, the pace of that motion has accelerated.

*As the energies carry you
to ever-higher levels of awareness,
your attunement to the higher frequencies becomes stabilized.
And the transition to an augmented perspective is achieved.*

*The transition to another level of reality
may not be apparent until it becomes obvious that
the rules of "the game"
have been radically altered.
Ultimately, one realizes that one is not now present
in the same world as one once was.*

*As your individual vibration accelerates in relation to
your dimension at large, your reality manifests, recognizably,
as a reflection of your choices.*

*As the time lag between the inception of thought
and the manifestation of reality diminishes,
it becomes obvious to you that
you are creating all of it.*

*As your journey toward Oneness accelerates,
your experience as a physical being takes on the breadth of perspective
and the heightened awareness characteristic of
the higher dimensions of existence.*

*Ascension is not something that is done to you.
It is a process that is initiated by you, orchestrated by you,
and experienced fully as an evolutionary journey by you.*

*Ascension is not a onetime hurdle
that, once traversed, is an event relegated to the past.
It is a never-ending process.
You are experiencing its effects
all the time.*

*Even though your reality, as you perceive it to be,
will remain as the "here and now,"
your sense of your self within this reality
expands in scope.*

*Your ascension into the range of realities
where you know yourself to be One with all else you encounter,
marks the turning point in your evolution
as a pinpoint of consciousness
with Self-perception.*

*The planet itself
is undergoing unprecedented changes in its energetic composition.
The life that is able to be sustained at each of the various levels
is affected accordingly.*

*Your physical realms
will not cease to exist in the world to come.
They simply will have experienced a spiritual transformation.
They will offer the spiritual travelers amongst you
a destination through which to rediscover
your Sacred Essence, in physical form,
under optimal conditions.*

Who Am I?

*You have awakened
in the middle of a never-ending dream.*

*In increments, you begin to experience a taste
of the magnitude of the real power
that is your true essence.*

*You have glimpsed yourself —
safe in the sanctity of all that swirls around you.
In all likelihood, you haven't remained in that sacred center
longer than a moment. But the realization registered nonetheless
that somewhere within the realm of possibility
there was that indescribable sense of peace.
And you recognized that state of Beingness —
for it is the nature of your own
very Essence.*

Despite evidence to the contrary,
you are none the worse for wear for having
lived through the symbolic earthquakes
of your personal life dramas.
If anything, your sense of resourcefulness has been strengthened.
Your resiliency has been reinforced.
And in the absence of much, if not all, of what you expected
you would be able to bank on,
something indestructible and timeless remained –
your own sacred essence.

Each blow to your pride, each disappointing outcome,
is no more than an instrument of your own will,
a symbolic prop with which you, as the consummate playwright,
sought to mirror yourself.

*Buried in the depths of your illusions,
far beneath the distortions of all you were taught to believe,
is a level of Self that would remain untouched.
It is that precious spark of your own Divinity
that you seek to discover, safe within you, when all else fails –
as you knew it would.
You were the one who set it up that way.*

*You may think
that the journey you have made
is yours, for your experience has told you so.
But in truth, your experience is
but a glimpse into the composite reality
that is the shared vision
of these times.*

You are not in this movie,
unless you choose to perceive yourself to be.
You are, in fact, watching it.

Leaving the Past Behind

*With the help of the energies
that flood your world,
you have been gifted with the experience
of a Divine moment.*

*Now, there is a chance to rise above
the conditions of experiential reprisal for choices made
in levels of reality that you would consider to be "the past."*

*Now, you have the chance to accelerate
a process of experiential compensation that, under denser conditions,
might have taken centuries.*

*For some, it is only when you are absolutely convinced
that you are hopelessly lost – when you simply do not know
where to turn – that you turn within,
and the real journey begins.*

*The power of guilt and fear
has continued to nourish the unrelenting sense of helplessness
with which many of you emerged into awareness in this reality.
Transcending that conditioning is a feat
not to be underestimated.*

*Your own interaction with your inner resistance
has kept you bound to the illusion of the old paradigm
and the gospel of limitation to which many of you were wedded.
It required the wrenching experiences of disillusionment
that you have weathered to break the bonds of some of those ties.*

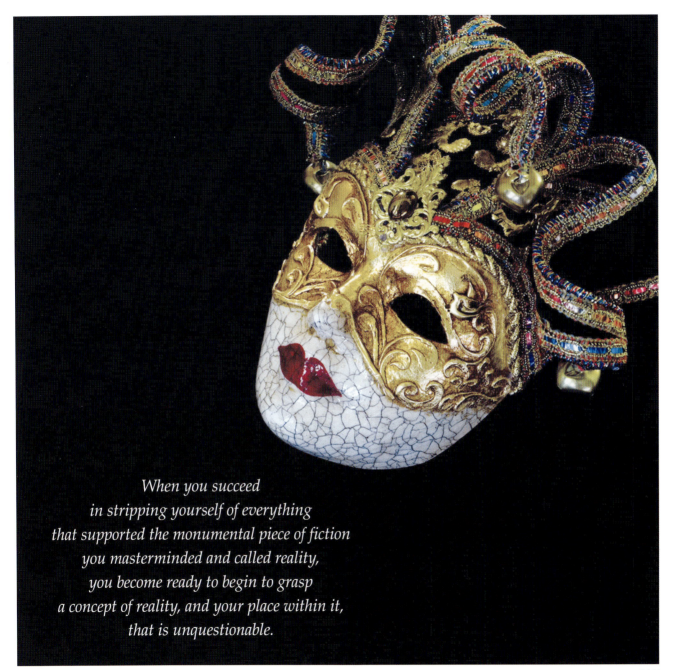

*When you succeed
in stripping yourself of everything
that supported the monumental piece of fiction
you masterminded and called reality,
you become ready to begin to grasp
a concept of reality, and your place within it,
that is unquestionable.*

*When, at last,
there is nothing left to lose,
you are ready.
For only then, in the sacred space of humility,
are you able to recognize and to embrace
what has never been lost.
That precious spark
awaits you.*

The Call of Divine Intent

*Never before
in the history of your world
has there been a time of transformation
such as this.*

*All Creation is engulfed
in the momentum of change.*

*All are experiencing
the integration of accelerated vibration –
and the wonders of
a new world of perception.*

*Your innate sensitivity and awareness
of the reality of the world beyond the material
has come to the forefront of the consciousness of humankind,
irrespective of differences in culture.*

*The call of the higher purpose
of Divine Intent
calls for a radical change in the ground rules
that govern physical reality.*

*The momentum
toward recognition of your mutual Oneness with each other
is not a new development that has been reserved for a "New Age."
This truth is the essence of the timeless –
the very foundation of All That Is.*

*In order that All Life
might partake of the opportunity to taste
their innate Divinity
and ultimately, to unite in Oneness,
it was necessary that certain conditions be altered
so that the energies of stagnation might be transcended
by those who were ready to be free.
That is the nature of the experience
of these times.*

Creating your Reality

*Recognizing the power to create your reality
is your key to turning the page
and beginning a new chapter in your own life story.*

*The tools for creating your personal reality
as a masterpiece of manifested intent
are right there within the parameters of
your consciousness.*

*The full thrust of one's intent draws into the arena of possibility
the circumstances that will carry the intent
through to manifestation.*

*Knowing now that all things are possible,
you are able to make significant choices and, at the same time,
you are able to take full responsibility for
the ramifications of those choices.*

*As the time lag between
the inception of thought and the manifestation of reality diminishes,
it becomes obvious to you that you are creating all of it.*

*One becomes the creator and the creation simultaneously.
And one is able to experience the fullness of limitless expression
as the embodiment of the harvest of all seeds sown.*

*With the newfound absence of limitation
comes the realization
that one must now take total responsibility
for the focused intent that underlies one's choices.
One can no longer take the default position
that one "has no choice" or that one was obliged
to select from a limited number of options
in any situation.*

*The process (of manifestation) is less a by-product of
making choices from a given number of possible options,
than of starting from a position of limitlessness
and drawing forth the corresponding options
as possibilities to be embraced
as choice.*

Once one has cleared the slate of the karmic vibrational remnants that once compromised one's energy field, there is literally nothing left with which to magnetize life experience other than the vibrational essence of what it is that you want.

*When you approach the process of manifestation
at the higher vibrational levels to which you now are ascending,
you are no longer afforded the luxury of passivity.*

*The old mode of operation
that may have seen you living your life with a "wait and see" approach,
will not manifest anything at the higher vibrational levels,
other than confusion.*

*The nature of your world is no more and no less than
a reflection of the composite vision
of the consciousness present.*

*It is entirely possible
to transcend a prophesied series of events
that once seemed so likely
as to have been considered inevitable.
There is no event that is so inevitable as to be resistant to
the focused intent of the beings present.*

Honoring your Inner Truth

*These times represent
an unprecedented crossroads for many.
For you have emerged in awareness at a place
where many worlds intersect.
Your perceptions, and the choices they prompt you to make,
will help to determine just how rocky
the climb ahead will be.*

*Those of you
who have reached a place of
inner surrender to the majesty of
what you have begun to experience – in your inner world –
will encounter the "path of least resistance"
which will lead you on the next leg of your journey.
You will recognize it, inwardly,
even though you may believe it to be "the great unknown."
For, the part of you
that has opened, at long last,
knows it well.*

*Do not expect
the inevitable conclusions
you will draw from your experiences
to "make sense."
Often, they will not. Not at first.
But slowly, all of it will emerge as crystalline clarity
when you surrender lifetimes of learned conditioning
to the unmistakable truth of
what you feel.*

*One's own experience
is far more significant proof of what is so
than platitudes of logic that one has learned to parrot,
and against which one's reality is often measured.
The nature of these changes transcends your so-called logic.
It is based on a blueprint of Divine intent
that is unquestionable.*

*The power of the consensus understanding
of what is real – and what is unreal –
is known to be irrelevant if it cannot be verified
by how it feels to you.*

Inner-knowingness
is being kindled within the consciousness
of every being throughout your world.
And as each of you instinctively begins to attune
to the higher resonance of that awareness,
the answers that were once elusive
emerge from within.

Suddenly, you know the answers
without even having formulated the question.
For, you will have tapped into profound levels of deeper understanding
that were unavailable to your conscious mind
at diminished levels of vibration.

Once your frequency stabilizes at the higher levels,
you will come into conscious awareness
of levels of understanding that were not formally learned.
Concepts take on a clarity and a breadth of vision
that cannot be justified
by linear logic.

*You become aware
that you have emerged as a very different kind of being,
for reasons you cannot explain.*

*The free-will
that is inherent in
the human condition
is unconditional.
You are free to do anything,
be anything,
and believe anything,
in any way it pleases you.
That is your God-given
birthright.
And with that freedom
goes the right
to reap the ramifications
of all actions.
You yourself
built that into the system,
so you would be able
to experience
the results
of your choices.*

*The opportunity
presented under the conditions of transition
is to recognize for oneself what is so – and to honor that truth,
even in the face of adversity.*

*Resist the temptation to be seduced by your own ego
in its need for validation.
For, the truth you seek lies not upon the path of another,
but within your personal process of emergence.*

*It is far more powerful to live your truth
than to preach it.*

*Teach by example
that which you are inclined to share.
For, your actions speak far more clearly than any theory
you may feel inspired to impart.
This is the strongest way
to impart the message you would most wish to have heard
by those who don't want to hear it.*

*For each of you,
there is only one truth: your truth.
It is contradictory to the very concept of spiritual devotion
to subscribe to a school of thought forced upon you
by the might of the masses,
when such concepts violate what you know to be
your own inner truth.*

*In order to be truly free
of the shackles of obligation
perpetrated upon so many of you,
it is necessary to shift one's loyalties.
Your obligation is not to the so-called "truth"
that may have been handed down through
generations of misguided seekers.
Your obligation is to the truth that has been unearthed
within the depths of your own heart –
and to that alone.*

Your Spiritual Path

*It matters less
what you may or may not have read,
or heard, or been taught as to what is the correct way
to proceed on the spiritual path,
than what your own experience
has shown you
to be so.*

*You are not required to select and to practice
a recognized spiritual discipline, or to subscribe to a religion,
in order to fully experience your sacred journey to Oneness.*

*You who have been humbled under the yoke of fear
into bearing the burden of the man-made dogmas of your world
have been given a convoluted detour,
rather than a direct path to the Divinity you seek.*

*You are not obligated to participate in rituals
simply because that is the heritage of your family in this lifetime.
Participate if it gives you pleasure to do so,
and you will have exercised
the highest choice.*

*It matters not whether you choose
to follow in the footsteps of your ancestors
in your expressions of devotion,
or upon a path that no one has ever walked before –
so long as your heart has led you to it.*

*The experience
of joyous Divine connectedness
transcends all barriers of culture and belief
and has been experienced, since time immemorial,
by beings of all backgrounds.*

*You have been given unlimited freedom of choice.
And that choice encompasses all avenues of the expression of
your innate Divinity.*

*The opportunity here,
in these times of blossoming self-awareness,
is to recognize the unlimited potential in who and what you are,
and to gift yourself with permission to express that knowingness
as you choose to.*

*The freedom to worship as you choose
is your God-given birthright.
There is no one who knows better than you do,
the devotional path
that is the most gratifying for you.*

*When one approaches any effort
with the energy of reluctance or half-heartedness,
the result will not be satisfying.*

*When you choose a spiritual path
because your mind tells you that you should,
you can expect to be disappointed.*

*The vibrancy of any approach
is based not on the mechanics of the spiritual practice,
but upon one's total surrender to the direction
in which the practice leads you.*

*The key to one's success or failure
at any given (spiritual) technique
has nothing whatsoever to do with the technique,
but rather, with the energy of joyousness
with which you approach it.*

*When one is present, in the moment,
in a state of heightened receptivity,
one adds the essential ingredient
to any spiritual practice.*

*The torchbearers of these times
who illuminate the path of others
do so in order to kindle the awareness of each
that the true path leads within.*

*The true teachers of your times
do not seek to be exalted in your eyes.
They have chosen to show you, by example,
the validity of a vision
in which each of you is exalted
in your own eyes.*

Unity with Diversity

*None of you is any different,
in your core essence, than any other.
You simply are here to hold a particular note in the resonance
that is playing as a particular symphony of experience:
this "here and now."
How you choose to experience that aspect of
the One Divine Presence
is totally up to you.*

*In your recognition of the truth of
your perspective on the experience of life,
you hold a priceless piece of the composite vision of reality.*

*Each of you holds a unique vision
and the experience of the Divine connectedness of each
is unparalleled.*

*You may describe your experience of awakening
with the same words as another being, or may find in hearing or reading
the words of another, that the sentiments expressed describe your own.
Yet language cannot begin to approximate
the essence of the experience itself.*

*The differences that divide you
are the very concepts that, ultimately,
you will embrace as a unified race of beings.
The momentum for the transcendence of those differences
is the hallmark of these times of transformation.*

*The countless differences in perspective amongst you
are not evidence of a world of falsehood, but rather are proof
of the infinite levels of Divine truth,
personified by the presence of each of you.*

*The contrast provided
by the mirror of the vision of another being
is the gift you bring one another,
in order that each of you may perceive his own vision more clearly.*

*If all were whistling the same one note,
there would be no music.*

*If all painted the canvas of their life's creation
with the same favorite color, the collective would be a bland vision
devoid of contrast or detail.*

*Your truth cannot be the truth of another being.
Each of you perceives the experience of life
through a lens that has been designed to deliver a vision
custom-made for your eyes only.*

The differing perceptions of another do not invalidate your own,
they merely add the richness of contrast
to the composite vision
that is Oneness.

The Artist & The Dreamer

*Your essential nature
is not focused in goal-oriented activity,
but is rooted in your feeling body – your emotions.
The drive you experience toward accomplishing a given end
is not based upon a need to fulfill a dream,
but rather, is based upon a need to avoid sliding
into the abyss of your fears.*

*In order to manifest
the world of The Artist,
it is necessary first to recreate
the world of The Dreamer.
This is the world of the eternal child,
into which you were born in this lifetime.
The child does not know the concept of limitation.
These are the shackles with which his world equips him.
In his dreams there are no limitations,
and his wishes and desires dominate
his every moment.*

*Before The Artist can begin
to emerge from the radiant core of your being
and give expression to the unique creation that is to be your life,
you must first find and liberate The Dreamer
from the prison
of your linear consciousness.*

*The Dreamer
is the glowing spark of joyousness
that somehow became buried beneath the burden
of all you have undertaken to do in this lifetime.
The Dreamer does not dwell in the realm of doing
but thrives in the innocence of
simply being.*

*The Dreamer does not care what is or is not possible.
For, the Dream is based in limitlessness.*

*The Dream is found
in the depths of the child who still dwells within.
Reconnecting with that rarefied spark of your own Divine essence
is the key element in restructuring the life
you are preparing to transform.*

*The Dreamer is set free
when you set aside the ego-focused priorities
with which you have tied your own hands and allow
your true essence to emerge.*

*The fresh innocence
of unbridled joy that you harbor within
cannot thrive in the structured conditions you created
in a world built on the premise of compromise.*

*It will be necessary to learn to distinguish,
within the context of your desires, between those that are based in fear
and those that stem from the innocence of the joyousness
that is your fundamental essence.*

*The sweetness
of the vision of The Dreamer, awaiting your rediscovery,
is the elusive missing piece
in your journey of self-discovery.*

The Journey Home

What you yearn to experience,
and fault the external trappings of your existence for not providing,
has been within you all along – waiting patiently.

*The moment for turning inward
announces its arrival blatantly –
in silence.*

*The vantage point
from which you are able to observe yourself in this moment
puts into perspective the rich and often rocky terrain you have traversed.*

*Had you not had the taste of the bitter as well as the sweet,
you would have emerged with a theoretical understanding,
supported only by your observations
of the trials and tribulations
in the lives of others.*

You have not failed yourself for
"having taken so long" in your journey of awakening.
For, the vantage point that awaits you at the summit of the mountain
would not have carried the impact that is possible
had you not made the arduous climb.

*There is no element of stature
or lack of stature on the spiritual journey.
For, All Is Oneness.
You each are simply at a different moment –
a split-second, freeze-action spark of awareness –
on a journey that is timeless.
The collective points of illumination
form the composite perspective of the journey
known as "enlightenment."*

*The present moment's clarity
does not invalidate the journey that was necessary
in order to attain it.*

*In order to avail yourself of the richness
in the experience of knowing your Divine connectedness,
it was necessary to avail yourself of the richly contrasting details of
the experience of separation.*

*You may think
that the journey you have made is yours
for your experience has told you so.
But, in truth, your experience is but a glimpse into
the composite reality that is the shared vision
of these times.*

You are never too busy, or too committed,
to pause and reconsider when life presents you with the possibility of
a radical turnabout in what you thought were your plans.
Those plans were merely the detour you used
to bring yourself to the moment where the real direction
might be stumbled upon
"by accident."

*Oneness
has no agenda
with regard to the timetable
of your transformation.
It does not matter
whether you embrace
who you really Are
this year —
or even in this lifetime.
For time, as it truly is,
has no relation to the illusions
in the linear dream
you call your life.*

*We are here,
waiting patiently for you,
as we have been for all eternity.
We are willing to wait ...*

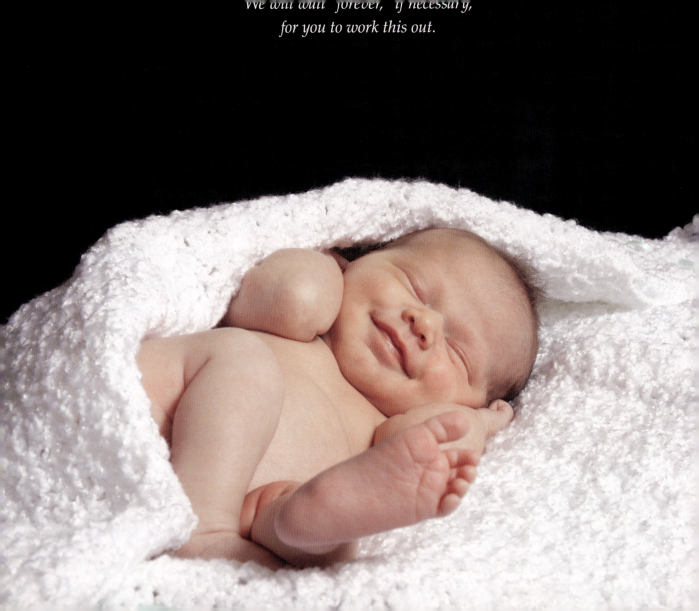

We will wait "forever," if necessary, for you to work this out.

*And if it takes forever,
you are no less
our Beloved.*

*You can surely protest
your spiritual innocence
long after the initiation of your heart.
But once awakened, your knowingness will not be forgotten.
It will resurface and nudge you into remembrance
when you least expect it to.
It will emerge with that familiar kindred glow –
just to remind you that
you have not been
forgotten.*

Compassion

*Compassion is the common thread
with which the tapestries of each of your lives are interwoven.
For, in truth, there Is only One of us here.*

*It is the Oneness in each of you
that recognizes the Oneness in another,
and unites you in a breath of harmony that is shared.
In each interaction, there is the promise of that attainment of balance,
even when one reaches out only by listening,
or simply by being there.*

You have built for yourself the foundation for
the experience of compassion
by having watched illustration after illustration
of your own worst fears come to life.

It is far easier to understand
the nature of another person's pain, having lived it yourself.
Having crawled out of the dark night of your own soul's journey,
it is easier for you to recognize the truth underlying
the nightmares of another.

*The experience of compassion
is one in which balance is sustained between
bonding and boundaries.
One is able to reach out and to care deeply for
the poignancy of another's process,
to recognize the underlying theme as a common thread
woven in your own experience,
and at the same time, to distance yourself, vibrationally,
from the heat of the blaze.*

*As you begin to recognize the parallels
in the lives of those with whom you share this dance,
you begin to recognize the uncanny perfection
in the synchronicity of the moments that bring you together.
It becomes blatantly obvious that there are
no random occurrences.*

*Know that in giving,
the giving is never one-sided.
For the giver is equally gifted
in ways you have only begun
to understand.*

*When compassion is expressed in earnest,
the burden is lightened for each of you.*

You are Oneness

*Oneness has chosen
to make this journey as each of you.
And we have done so – you have done so –
in order to know yourself in the fullness of All That Is,
having had the experience of it.*

Your own exalted moments of awakening
add a brilliant note to the indescribable harmony being co-created,
as each of you add your resonance to
the multidimensional whole.

*Yours is a world
in which you ultimately
distance yourself,
emotionally,
from everything
you ever held dear,
in an effort
to avoid
further pain.
Ultimately,
you distance yourself
from yourself.
You set to one side
everything
that has characterized
the identity
you invested a lifetime
in creating.
For, at last,
this mask
has ceased to be
recognizable to you
as yourself.*

*You are no more or less who you now are
than all the masks you have worn and all the posturing
you have demonstrated along the way.
All of it are integral parts of an identity that seeks resolution,
not in the act of discarding what was,
but in the act of integrating all of it into
the composite of what Is.*

*The opportunity
for you who are moving through
this experience of transcendence with your eyes wide open
is to see that the concept of unification in Oneness
is not to be interpreted in a physical sense.
It is an experiential journey.*

*All the illustrious past lives,
who have shared this lifetime, are within you.
As are the future selves who act out the scripts
you believe to be yet unwritten.
All are within you – harbored in the sacred core
of your Eternal Being.*

*You cannot hope to ascend
into the embrace of the higher energies
with a whitewashed identity and gaping holes in your history.
The aspects of self that await your imminent arrival
do not hope for part of you.
They are waiting patiently for all of you.
And the fragments of your identity that you'd rather not look at,
are the ones most needed in your loving embrace.*

*Here, in the aftermath of
the great shedding of one's outgrown skin,
you now find yourself. And the temptation is great
to cast the scraps of all that once was valid and meaningful
into the trash, and to turn your back and walk away.
Ah! If only it were that simple.
But, naturally, it's not.
The object of this exercise is Oneness – not separation.
And that includes Oneness with
all you have ever been.*

You have connected with the timeless.
You have opened to the possibility of transcending
all that defines your existence —
and the world that gives it
definition and form.

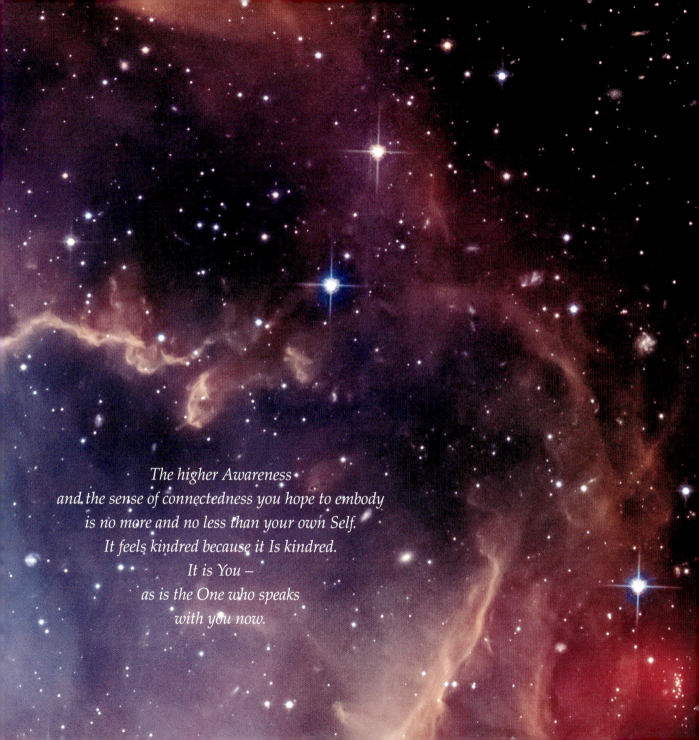

*The higher Awareness
and the sense of connectedness you hope to embody
is no more and no less than your own Self.
It feels kindred because it Is kindred.
It is You –
as is the One who speaks
with you now.*

*In embracing the inner glow of recognition of
the kindredness of the most intangible connection of all,
you take the quantum leap.*

Enlightenment

*There is no
static condition
of enlightenment
on the path of enlightenment.
It is an ongoing journey
that continues
to evolve.*

*There is nothing foreign or otherworldly
about experiencing your connectedness with God.
For, it is none other than your very own Divine essence,
ever-present within you, that reaches out in that embrace.
It is not something that suddenly enters.
It is something that has never left.*

*When you have experienced
the harmony of that heart-felt glow,
even for a fleeting moment,
the knowingness is indelibly etched upon your consciousness.
And that level of knowingness cannot be forgotten.*

*Once you are able to look at another being
and see no difference at all, there is no need for harmony.
For here, there Is only Oneness.
This is the place the story began. And this is the end
toward which all consciousness
now strives to return.*

*You are destined to transcend the need for harmony
and to experience the essence of Isness
in unison with All Life.*

*Each of you will remain
in a state of self-perception for all eternity.
And as you enter the states of higher awareness,
each of you will be graced with Self-Perception.
That is the essence of Oneness.
We are the essence of
each of you.*

*No matter how
you manifest your emergence
into the next level of awareness that awaits you,
there will be no question that your journey is perfection.
Through the eyes of Oneness,
that is the only possibility.
And those are the eyes through which
you have witnessed
all of it.*

*It is You
who will have created this world anew,
by recognizing yourself as Oneness –
and resonating as One.
Just as it was ...
In The Beginning.*

Acknowledgements and Image Credits

My deepest appreciation to the extraordinary metaphorical artist, **Vladimir Kush,** *for the use of his breath taking painting, "Pearl," as the cover image for this book.*
www.vladimirkush.com

My heartfelt gratitude to the gifted photographers who so graciously gave their permission for the use of the following images in this volume:

Daniel Endy – pp. 15, 19, 97, 98, 162, 178, 181, 201

Mary Josephine Hession – pp. 44, 73, 104, 168, 176

Randall Collis – p. 151 – www.dalocollis.com

Tim Kemple – pp. 76 - 77

Seth Bullington – pp. 89, 102

Bernd Kalidas Flory – p. 79

Dev Gogoi – p. 120 - 121 – www.devgogoi.wordpress.com

Jason Ware – p. 14 – www.galaxyphoto.com jw_POSS_plus_meade_m31_fin1

My heartfelt thanks to the gifted graphic designer, **S. Janarthanan,** *at Prisma in Auroville, Puducherry, India for the blessing of his talent and artistry in the design and production of this book. Jana, it's been such a privilege to work with you!*

My thanks to the **Chandra Observatory/NASA** *(USA) for their permission to use the following images in this volume:*

p. 93 – "Galactic Pyrotechnics on Display" NGC 4258 – *Image credit:* X-ray: NASA/CXC/Caltech/P. Ogle et al; Optical: NASA/STScI; IR: NASA/JPL-Caltech; Radio: NSF/NRAO/VLA

p. 186 – "Antennae"
Image Credit: NASA, ESA, and the Hubble Heritage Team (STScI/AURA)

p. 90 – MACSJ0717
Image Credit: X-ray: NASA/CXC/IfA/C. Ma et al. Optical: NASA/STScI/IfA/ C.Ma et al.

p. 208 - 209 – NGC 602a
Image Credit: X-ray: NASA/CXC/Univ.Potsdam/L. Oskinova et al; Optical: NASA/STScI; Infrared: NASA/JPL-Caltech

My thanks to **La Silla/ESO** *– European Southern Observatory (Chile) for their permission to use the following images in this volume:*

p. 218 – "Helix Nebula" NGC 7293
Image Credit: ESO

p. 145 – "The Orion Nebula" ESO 1103a
Image Credit: ESO/Igor Chekalin

Rasha
August, 2015

About Rasha

Author of the spiritual classic, *Oneness*, Rasha awakened to her inner calling as a Messenger of Divine guidance in 1987. She began working with Oneness, the Divine Presence we all share, in 1998, documenting the Revelations that serve as the foundation for her work. In the process, she was taken step by step through the sacred journey to Oneness and through the life-altering changes that are shaking the foundation of today's world.

As a spiritual teacher with a profound message, Rasha is not affiliated with any established spiritual path, religion or guru. The teachings she transcribes are universal and focus on the experience of the Divinity within each of us, and the profound transformation of consciousness that is the hallmark of these times.

American by birth, Rasha now lives at the foot of the mystical mountain, Arunachala, in South India. There, cloistered in blessed silence, life is filled with the joy of transcribing the words of Oneness for future volumes.

More Divine Wisdom from Earthstar Press:

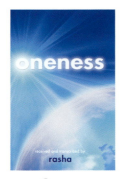

Oneness
ISBN: 987-0-965900317

Oneness - Audio Book
16-CD Set
ISBN: 987-0-965900331

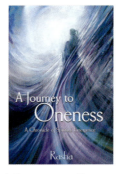

A Journey to Oneness
ISBN: 978-0-965900348

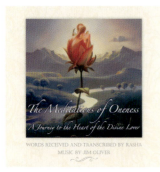

The Meditations of Oneness - CD
UPC: 884501255172

Oneness - Audio Book
MP3 2-CD Set
ISBN: 978-0965900324

The Calling
ISBN: 978-0965900300

For more information about
the teachings of Oneness through Rasha visit:
www.onenesswebsite.com
Contact: onenessmailbox@gmail.com

Facebook: www.facebook.com/Oneness.through.Rasha
www.facebook.com/onenessspeaks